Index

Foreword

<u>Some key themes and principles running through this book.</u>

My book aims to be the key that unlocks your understanding and potential so you can get the most out of dance classes, lessons, social dances and YouTube presentations etc.

How to do dance moves is standard practice, how to interpret this standard practice is what my book is about.

I have deliberately picked similar dance moves, and description styles on how to execute the moves, to show patterns and links. Other books concentrate on the technical side of dancing, whereas my book emphasises the pattern/spirit in easy-to-remember key points. It also includes technical information on how to improve your dancing as you gain experience.

There are many and varied dance steps which can be performed in a variety of holds, too many for me to mention all of them in this book. So I have focused on a select few as a quick-start guide to dancing. Once you have tried them in the order I have suggested, you can fit them together in different combinations.

The box below is what a Goddard tip looks like – where you see one, it is one of my key things to remember, to help you improve your dancing.

> All dances start with Leader's right foot and Follower's left foot except the Jive and Tango. These start with Leader's left foot and Follower's right foot.

Chapter 1 Sharing my Dance Experiences and Introducing the Goddard Method of Ballroom and Latin Dancing

Dancing is Fun - Let's enjoy it together

The reason I wrote this book is that people can get overwhelmed with the level of detail in lessons, books and YouTube videos. I want to get across to readers an executive summary level of detail; so I have written instructions that break down dances into bite-size chunks to help you better understand what you are doing when taking lessons, looking at reference guides or perhaps learning new moves with a partner.

Dancing is a continuous journey of life-long learning. This book will give you the information you need regardless of whether you are a complete beginner or an experienced dancer.

When attending dances and dance classes, I have noticed that people have the same issues, regardless of how long they have been dancing:

Too much focus on 'what' to do, not enough on 'when' and 'how'.

My instructions will show you 'what', 'how' and 'when'; plus the key principles you need to know to make techniques work.

My aim is to give you advice, encouragement and guidance on how to do everything; from taking your first steps on the dance floor, to improving your technique - even after years of practice.

You'll find information on:

- What you need to know to get started – where to go, what to

wear, and so on.
- Basic dance steps - first step guides for Ballroom and Latin.
- More advanced dance steps - guides to taking things further.
- Technical points – to really help you improve your dancing.

Are you ready? Let's get started!

Chapter 2 Before You Start Dancing

What should I wear?

There is no dress code for lessons, wear something comfortable. You don't have to wear any special clothing or dance shoes. 'Sensible' shoes that can be worn in an office are entirely suitable.

The dress code for dances will be set out on advertising information. Most are smart-casual, but some may be black tie and formal dress (frock) affairs.

Why not see what bargains you can find in your local charity shop?

Dancing can be strenuous exercise, so you may wish to bring some spare clothes (such as a change of shirt for men) to classes or dances, particularly in hot weather.

Once you have tried lessons (or social dances) for some months and decided that you want to continue, that is the time to invest in some dance shoes.

Where can I dance?

There will be a dance class or a dance happening in your area. Look out for adverts on noticeboards, websites and social media.

What music will I dance to?

If it has a beat, you can dance to it. Different dances will require different styles of music from old school (eg Rat Pack) to modern (eg Ed Sheeran).

Chapter 3 What is Dancing?

Dancing is walking to music. A common mistake in dancing is trying to move unnaturally (eg stiffly) whilst looking at one's feet and leaning on someone else. When dancing, move naturally as you would when walking with a friend:

- Fall into step and go to the same place at the same time.
- Move in the same general direction as other people.
- Don't barge into others.
- Don't expect other people to prop you up. (Stand upright, don't lean on the other person.)

Below are some guides on what you need to know before you start Ballroom and Latin dancing.

- How to Dance:

    - First Principles
    - Second Principles

- Direction of Travel
- Dance Framework
- Leading and Following
- Dance Positions
- Ballroom and Latin Dances – The Key Steps

How to Dance?

The human body can only work efficiently in a limited number of ways. Martial arts, sports (eg swimming and running), yoga and dancing all have similar principles of movements. Once you can identify these patterns/principles it's possible to learn a new discipline quickly by applying what you know in a new way.

How to Dance: First Principles

- Avoid going off the edge of the dance floor.
- Go in the same direction as other couples.
- Avoid other dancers.
- If someone lifts an arm, turn under it. (It will almost always be the Follower who turns in basic moves, but can be the Leader in more advanced ones.)
- Hold onto your partner (but not too tightly); go where they go, when they move.

How to Dance: Second Principles

In order to dance you will need to:

- Learn the correct steps.
- Dance the correct steps to the correct rhythm.
- Dance the correct steps to the correct rhythm, whilst leading or following.

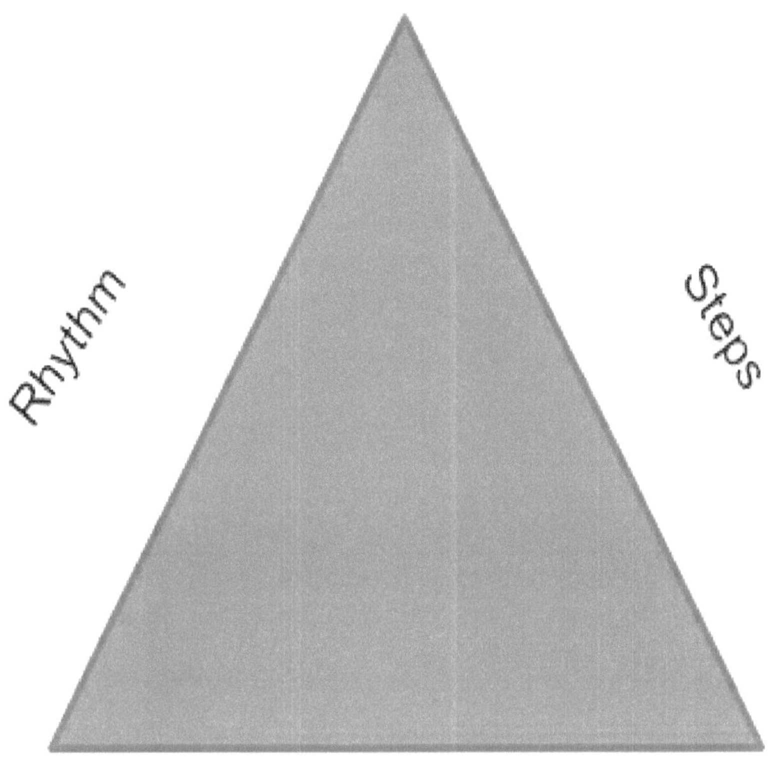

Take away any one of the above and the pyramid (ie dance) collapses.

Direction of Travel

How do I know which way to go?

As a rule of thumb:

- Ballroom – Start near a corner then follow along a wall anti-clockwise around the dance floor to the next corner.

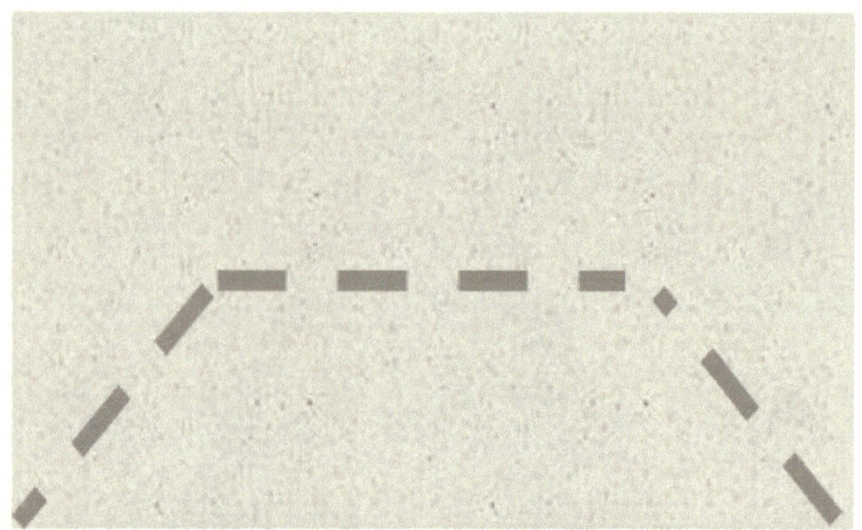

Throughout the book I will show direction of travel in pictures like the one above. The grey area represents the dance floor and dotted lines show your direction of travel.

- Latin – You generally stay in one place, at least for moves in this book (except for the Paso Doble.) There can be some travel in dances like the Samba when using more advanced moves eg *Running Promenades*.

Latin moves can be done anywhere on the dance floor so pictures do not show the whole dance floor as a reference point.

Dance Framework

Dancing is like driving a car:

- Two people get in a <u>**car**</u> to <u>**travel**</u> to the **same place** at the **same time**.
- Two people get in a <u>**framework**</u> to <u>**dance**</u> to the **same place** at the **same time**.

The Leader is responsible for:

- Direction.
- Power.

- Control.

The Follower:

- Responds to signals from the Leader.
- Helps to provide the momentum for dance steps.
- Mirrors the Leader's style eg arm positions.

Working equally together the **Leader and Follower make up the framework** to give it **strength** and **smooth lines**.

> It is important that the Leader and Follower maintain a smooth relationship during the dance.

When done correctly, dancing should look/feel a smooth, flowing and effortless movement. Everything will come together – moves, rhythm and working in partnership with the person you are dancing with.

Over time dancers put less reliance on sense of sight and more on their sense of touch to maintain the framework. In other words, less emphasis on watching what you are doing and more on connecting with your partner to get the smooth flow of the dance.

All dance steps shown in this book are performed in the standard 'teapot' hold (framework) unless indicated otherwise.

The framework is called 'teapot' as one arm is bent and the other more or less straight, but this can vary in position for Latin dances.

This is a typical Ballroom framework (no gap between dancers' bodies).

This is a typical Latin framework (gap between dancers' bodies).

Leading and Following

In order to dance well with someone, you need to get into the **correct hold** (using the previously mentioned 'teapot' framework) and then **lead** or **follow** once the dance starts.

Body contact is vital for leading or following.

Think about your partner's steps, not just your own, this will give them time to recover/re-centre after each move.

<u>Ballroom</u>

How to maintain contact:

- Form a framework of three points of contact: hand, arm and body (diaphragm to waist, partners almost face each other, but are off-centre so they look over each other's right shoulder).
- Maintain the framework (Leader and Follower hold on to each other) for the entire dance.
- Follower moves after Leader's hip starts moving but before Leader's foot lands.
- Leader steps forward (and maintains body contact), Follower steps back.
- Leader steps back, the Follower steps forward (and does so fast/far enough to maintain body contact).

Gapping can be a major problem in Ballroom as it will prevent two people dancing together

Gapping occurs when:

- Body contact is lost.
- Neither (or only one) party takes big enough steps.
- Both (or only one) party looks down to watch his/her feet.

<u>Latin</u>

How to maintain contact:

- A framework of two points of contact (hand and arm).
- Maintain the framework (Leader and Follower hold on to each other) for the entire dance.

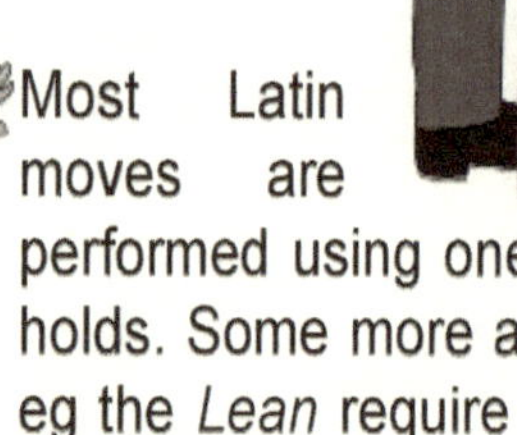

Most Latin moves are performed using one or two-handed holds. Some more advanced moves eg the *Lean* require body contact in the framework. So you may briefly need to use Ballroom framework principles (set out above) in your Latin dance.

<u>How to Lead and Follow</u>

People often mistakenly refer to "man" and "woman" steps. The correct terms are "Leader" and "Follower" which puts a different emphasis on how people should behave. At the very least, you need a business relationship that lasts as long as two people dance together.

The relationship is more like:

- Sender and receiver of information.
- A partnership between two equal partners. Both should put the same amount of effort into the framework/dance.
- One person leads and the other follows.
- There should be smooth movement; no pushing or shoving.

To draw a comparison between driving and dancing:

- When driving one looks in the mirror, signals then manoeuvres.
- When dancing:

    - The Leader should choose a move, signal to the Follower which move is required (by change of framework hold and/or hand grip), then perform the move.

    - The Follower should wait for the Leader to signal which move is required (by change of framework hold and/or hand grip), interpret the signal then react by performing the move.

<u>The Follower should not lead.</u>

<u>Signals</u>

There are many and varied signals given by Leaders to Followers. These can be learnt over time. A key principle to remember is that each of the following is a signal:

- Framework.

    - Different moves are used in each position when the Follower is on the Leader's side, behind or in front of the Leader.
    - Which hand the Leader uses to hold the Follower. This can be a one-handed, two-handed or cross-grip (eg Leader's right to Follower's right). Holds will vary between Ballroom and Latin dances.

- Direction of travel.

- Starting foot for a move – this signals direction of travel.
- Whether the Leader is upright (usually to travel) or leaning (usually to turn).

Every dance move in Ballroom and Latin has a different hold/grip. Sometimes it is a combination of factors that make the signal eg hand grip and direction of travel. For example, the *New York* and *Hand to Hand* step (Chapter 5) can start from the same foot position and hold, but direction of travel is signalled by the Leader to the Follower in order to distinguish the moves.

If couples do not dance in the correct framework for Ballroom or Latin, they will find it hard to send/receive signals ie lead or follow.

Remember the phrase "*lead from the heart*"? If the Leader leads from the diaphragm to waist area, this will give a clear movement signal to the Follower for both Ballroom and Latin dances.

Dance Positions

There are only seven dance positions that a Leader and Follower can adopt if they dance correctly. It is possible to use different moves and frameworks in each position. For instance, *position two* (Follower on Leader's left side) can be used for a *Hand to Hand* in Rumba or a *Bump* in the Jive. I have chosen just one move as an example in each of the illustrations below.

I have grouped the dance positions into rankings of one to five depending on their frequency of usage. First position is frequently used (if in doubt, go back to this unless another clear signal has been given), fifth position is used much less frequently. Frequency of use for other positions is somewhere between the two.

There can be one or two positions in each rank. If two, they are generally used equally.

Dance Position	Description	Exampl

First	Ballroom: Leader and Follower stand navel to navel, but off-centre (right side to right side instead of facing each other) eg standard Waltz position.	
	Latin: Leader and Follower face each other chest to chest standing roughly 30cm apart eg standard Samba position.	
Second	Follower on Leader's left side eg *Bump* in the Jive.	
	Follower on Leader's right side eg *Coca Rolas* in the Jive.	
Third	Follower on Leader's front diagonal left side eg *Under Arm Turn* in the Cha Cha Cha.	
	Follower on Leader's front diagonal right side eg *Hockey Stick* in the Rumba.	
Fourth	Follower behind Leader's back (both facing forwards) eg *Turkish Towel* in the Cha Cha Cha.	
Fifth	Follower in front of Leader	

	(both facing forwards) eg *Sliding Doors* in the Rumba.	

Ballroom and Latin Dances – The Key Steps

A journey of a thousand miles starts with the first step ….

So, how to dance Ballroom and Latin? What are the key steps for each dance?

A lot of people worry about the detail: What steps should I do and in which order?

The key to Ballroom and Latin dancing is to remember:

- A Waltz just requires you to **Step > Side > Close.**
- **Step > Side > Close > Side** will get you around the floor for the following dances:

  - Quickstep
  - Social Foxtrot

- Variation on **Step > Side > Close** or **Step > Side > Close > Side** (eg **Step > Rock > Side > Close > Side**) will get you around the floor for the following dances:

  - Cha Cha Cha
  - Jive
  - Rumba
  - Samba
  - Slow Foxtrot
  - Viennese Waltz

- (Basic level) Tango and Paso Doble just require you to **walk in time to the music**.

> It is worth practising these steps so you are confident in these manoeuvres / sequences.

> A '*step*' is generally the Leader's shoulder width for slow counts or a half shoulder width for quick counts.

There are other steps you can learn which differ from the above, but these foundation steps will get you around the dance floor.

How to Step – The Detail You Need to Know

This is one of the key themes I want to get across in my book. Correct footwork can make or break your dancing.

Reminder: The length of stride (how far you step) for both dancers is roughly equivalent to the Leader's shoulder width.

The stepping leg should move roughly thirty-five degrees to the supporting leg when stepping forward, back or sideways.

<u>Ballroom</u>

As a rule of thumb, step forward on a heel, other steps will be on the balls of your feet. The exception to this is Tango (see details later in book).

The illustration below sets out how to **Step > Side > Close.**

	Starting position.
	Supporting leg is straight down (Leader's left, Follower's right). Stepping leg is straight out (Leader's right, heel on ground; Follower's left, toe on ground).

	Having stepped: Weight is on Leader's right leg, so left is free to move. Weight is on Follower's left leg, so right is free to move.
	Weight is on Leader's left leg, so right is free to move, toe is touching floor. Weight is on Follower's right leg, so left is free to move, toe is touching floor.
	Leader drags right foot to close with left. Shift balance onto right leg to start a new step on left leg. Follower drags left foot to close with right. Shift balance onto left leg to start a new step on right leg.

Think of **Step > Side > Close** as **Down > Up > Up:** heel, toe (ball of foot to be precise) toe. Likewise, **Step > Side > Close > Side** is **Down > Up > Up > Up**.

Latin

Perform Latin dances on the balls of your feet. Like a boxer! Steps are generally much smaller than in Ballroom where you stride across the floor.

Chapter 4 Basic Ballroom Steps

Don't be misled by labels of *beginner*, *improver*, *intermediate* etc. No step is more important than the one you are doing now (when dancing). If anything, beginner moves are the most important as they lay the foundations for future moves to build on.

This chapter sets out a series of guides to help you start Ballroom dancing.

- Waltz
- Viennese Waltz
- Quickstep
- Slow and Social Foxtrot
- Tango

> You can refresh your memory about framework, leading and following by looking at details in Chapter 3 before going dancing.

> Reminder: All dances start with Leader's right foot and Follower's left foot except the Jive and Tango. These start with Leader's left foot and Follower's right foot.

How to Dance the Waltz - Change Step

Framework and Movement				
Follower Steps				
Timing	0	1	2	3
Steps		Step	Side	Close
Leader Steps				

As a rule of thumb, Followers go backwards as Leaders go forwards (and vice versa). Step > Side > Close is all you need to get around the room (until you learn more advanced steps).

To make things easy when you first start dancing the Waltz, I suggest Followers walk backwards as Leaders walk forwards, gradually turn in a circle as you dance anti-clockwise around the room. (Ant-clockwise is the direction of travel regardless of the step you use eg *Natural Turn or Reverse Turn* etc.)

As you get more confident, try adding other moves such as the *Box Step* (see below) to your dance.

As a rule of thumb, the full Waltz routine is: Turn > Turn > Straight. IE *Natural Turn > Change Step > Reverse Turn > Change Step >*

Box Step

Movement:

1. (Leader forward and Follower back) Step > Side > Close.
2. (Leader back and Follower forward) Step > Side > Close.

It's possible to *Box Step* clockwise and anti-clockwise. I suggest putting a *Change Step* between moves such as *Box Step* or *Natural/Reverse Turn*. The general direction of travel should be anti-clockwise around the room.

Natural Turn

Doing *Natural* and *Reverse Turns* will feel like doing a couple of three-point turns in a car.

Part	Timing	Leader's Steps	Follower's Steps
Natural Turn (clockwise) part 1	1	Step (forward and turn)	Step (backward and turn)
	2	Side	Side
	3	Close	Close
Natural Turn (clockwise) part 2	1	Step (backward and turn)	Step (forward and turn)
	2	Side	Side
	3	Close	Close
Change Step	1	Step (straight line)	Step (straight

		line)	
	2	Side	Side
	3	Close	Close

Reverse Turn

Part	Timing	Leader's Steps	Follower's Steps
Reverse Turn (anti-clockwise) part 1	1	Step (forward and turn)	Step (backward and turn)
	2	Side	Side
	3	Close	Close
Reverse Turn (anti-clockwise) part 2	1	Step (backward and turn)	Step (forward and turn)
	2	Side	Side
	3	Close	Close
Change Step	1	Step (straight line)	Step (straight line)
	2	Side	Side
	3	Close	Close

Whisk, Chasse and Half Natural Turn

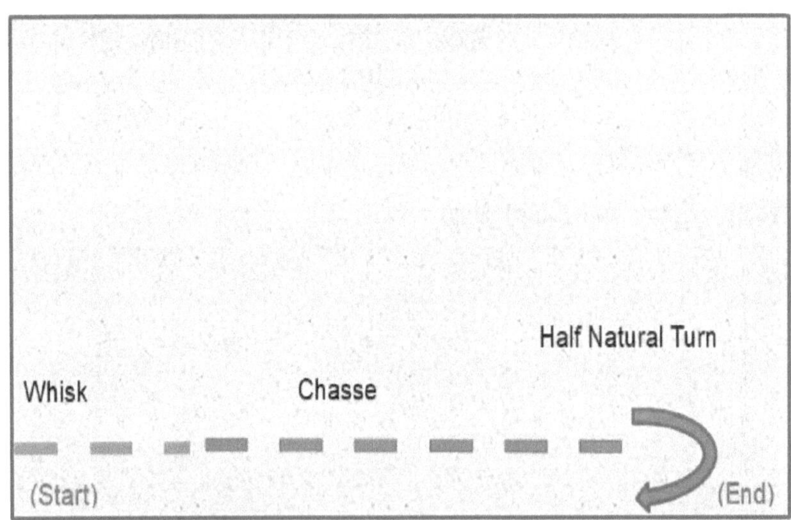

Part	Steps	Timing	When to do
Whisk	Step	Slow (1)	Following along wall
	Side	Slow (2)	
	Step behind (Leader's left behind right foot, Follower's right behind left foot)	Slow (3)	
Chasse	Step (Leader's right, Follower's left)	Slow (1)	Following along wall
	Side	Quick (2)	
	Close	Quick (and)	
	Side	Quick (3)	

Half Natural Turn	Step	Slow (1)	Near corner
	Side	Slow (2)	
	Close	Slow (3)	

Waltz: V4 (Spin Turn & Lock Step)

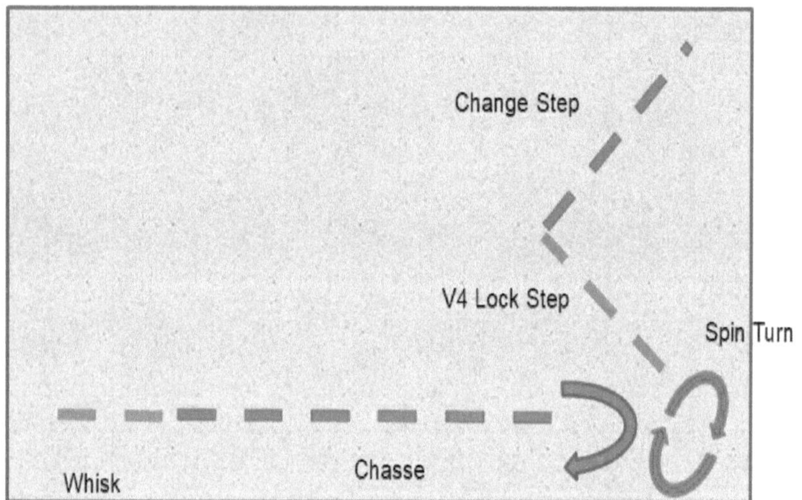

Part	Steps	Timing	When to do
Half Natural Turn	Step	Slow (1)	Near corner
	Side	Slow (2)	
	Close	Slow (3)	
Spin Turn	Step	Slow (1)	In corner
	Turn (turn 385 degrees and head away from corner into centre of dance floor)	Slow (2)	

	Step	Slow (3)	
V4	Step	Slow (1)	Away from corner
	Cross	Quick (2)	
	Step	Quick (and)	
	Step	Slow (3)	
Change Step	Step	Slow (1)	Towards next corner
	Side (turn 90 degrees anti-clockwise)	Slow (2)	
	Close	Slow (3)	

Key Principles for Dancing the Viennese Waltz

1. You can use a lot of your Ballroom Waltz steps in the Viennese Waltz, just adapt the rhythm and length of step.

   - Ballroom Waltz: Equidistant steps.
   - Viennese Waltz: Travel > Step on spot > Step on spot.

     - A *Lock Step* is needed alternatively by the Leader then Follower during *Reverse Turns* (instead of step on spot).

2. Foundation steps: Turn > Turn > Straight.
3. Some people say "I cross" (Leader) then "you cross" (Follower) to help them remember when to *Lock Step* on a *Reverse Turn*.
4. Lean into (*Natural/Reverse*) turns, be upright when going straight (*Change Steps*).
5. General direction of travel should be anti-clockwise around the

room.

Suggested Routine

Natural Turn (parts 1 and 2) > *Travelling Change Step* > *Reverse Turn* (parts 1 and 2) > *Travelling Change Step*.

Natural Turn

Part	Timing	Leader's Steps	Follower's Steps
Natural Turn (clockwise) part 1	1	Step (forward and turn)	Step (backward and turn)
	2	Side	Side
	3	Close	Close
Natural Turn (clockwise) part 2	1	Step (backward and turn)	Step (forward and turn)
	2	Side	Side
	3	Close	Close
Change Step	1	Step (straight line)	Step (straight line)
	2	Side	Side
	3	Close	Close

The **Side > Close** is on the same spot as where you land from the **Step.**

Reverse Turn

Part	Timing	Leader's Steps	Follower's Steps
Reverse Turn (anti-clockwise) part 1	1	Step (forward and turn)	Step (backward and turn)
	2	Side	Side
	3	Cross feet	Close
Reverse Turn (anti-clockwise) part 2	1	Step (backward and turn)	Step (forward and turn)
	2	Side	Side
	3	Close	Cross feet
Change Step	1	Step (straight line)	Step (straight line)
	2	Side	Side
	3	Close	Close

To summarise:

- Leader crosses feet.
- Follower crosses feet.
- No crossed feet.

Advanced Steps

Rather than always doing **Turn > Turn > Straight**, you can do four *Turns* then a *Change Step*. That is, do turns in multiples of twos then straighten up and change direction.

- Keep in contact.
- Remember to 'lead' and 'follow'.
- You will alternate between big and small steps like in the Waltz (don't keep them all the same size). For example, (big) Leader/(small) Follower steps > (small) Leader/(big) Follower steps.
- Each party will have to rotate around the other, which requires lots of torque (for power).

How to Dance the Quickstep

Part	Leader Steps	Follower Steps	Timing	Variations	
1	Step forward (right foot)	Step backward (left foot)	Slow	Use part 1 only	Use parts 1, 2 and 3
	Side	Side	Quick		
	Close	Close	Quick		
	Side	Side	Slow		
2	Step backward	Step forward	Slow		
	Side	Side	Quick		
	Close	Close	Quick		
	Side	Side	Slow		
3	Step forward (right foot)	Step backward	Slow		

	(left foot)		
Step forward (left foot)	Step backward (right foot)	Quick	
Close right foot behind left	Cross left foot over right	Quick	
Step forward (left foot)	Step backward (right foot)	Slow	

To avoid tripping over, cross in front when doing a backwards *Lock Step*, and cross behind when doing a forwards *Lock Step*.

Direction of Travel 1

Using steps from variation 1, you can move up, across and down the dance floor.

Leader and Follower should face one another.

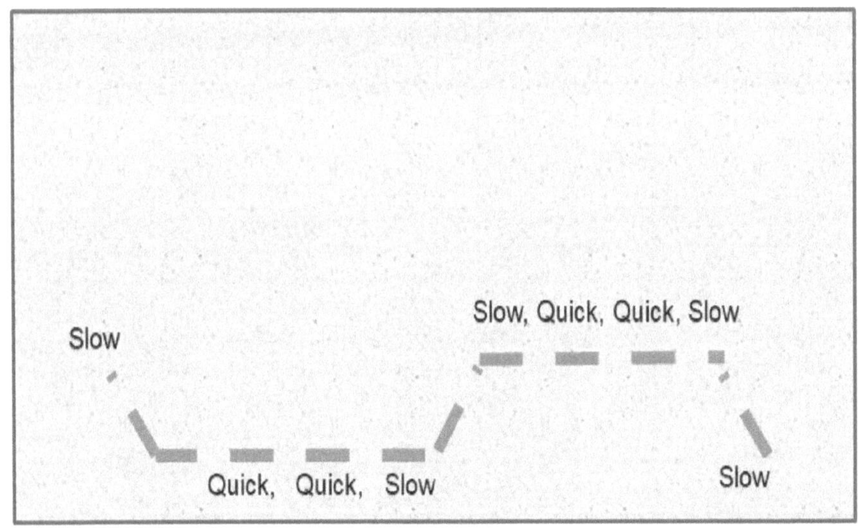

Quickstep: Direction of Travel 2

Using steps from variation 2 (*Basic Step* and *Lock Step*):

- Parts 1 & 2 - move up, across and down the dance floor.

    - Leader and Follower should face one another.

- Part 3 - move diagonally.

    - Leader beside Follower on his/her right side.

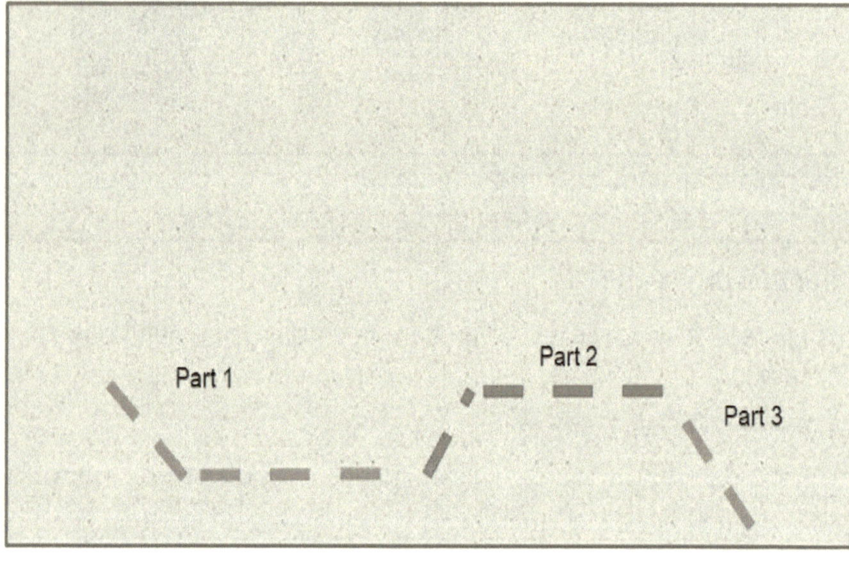

Quickstep: V6 (Spin Turn & Lock Step)

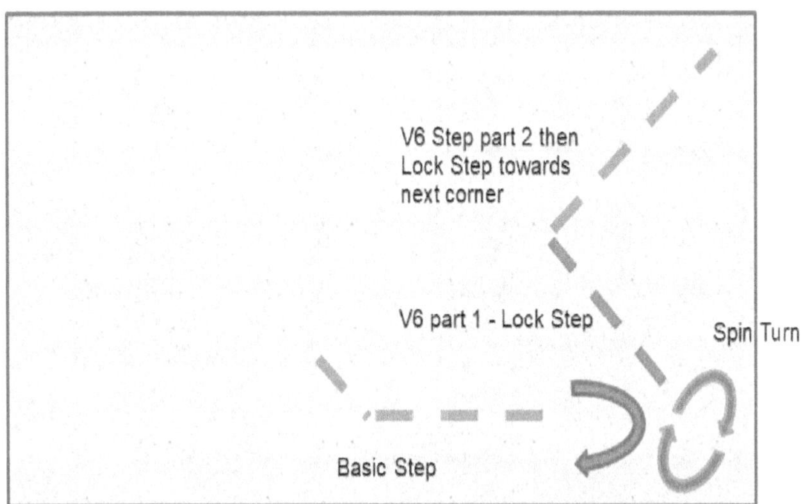

Quickstep: V6 (Spin Turn & Lock Step)

Part	Steps	Timing	When to do
Basic Step	Step	Slow	Following along wall
	Side	Quick	
	Close	Quick	
	Side	Slow	
Half Natural Turn	Step	Slow	Near corner
	Side	Quick	
	Close	Quick	
Spin Turn	Step	Slow	In corner
	Turn (turn 385	Slow	

	degrees and head away from corner into centre of dance floor)		
	Step	Slow	
V6	Step	Slow	Away from corner
	Cross	Quick	
	Step	Quick	
	Step	Slow	
	Step and contract	Quick	Towards next corner
	Step and turn/bounce	Quick	

Do you remember the *V4* in the Waltz? The *V6* in the Quickstep works on a similar principle.

The *V4* is usually finished with a *Change Step*. The V6 is usually finished with a *Lock Step*.

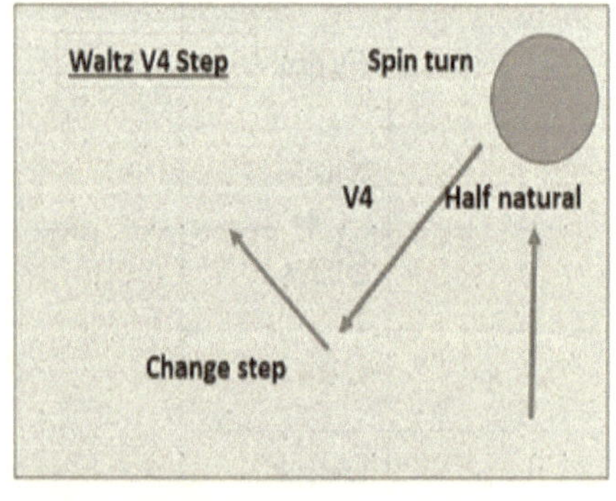

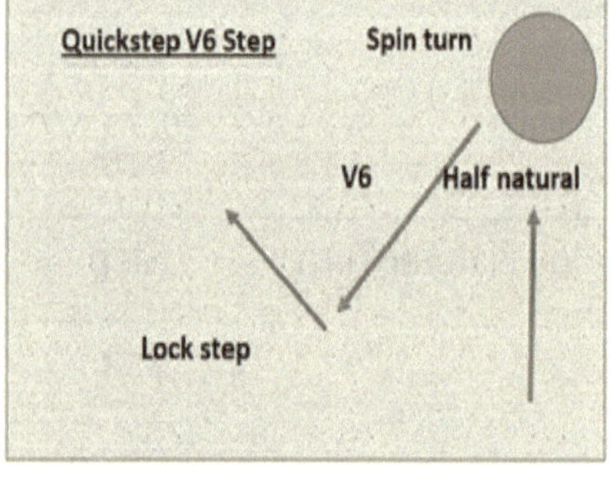

V4:

Speed	Slow,	Quick,	Quick,	Slow
Timing	1		2	3

V6:

Speed	Slow, Quick, Quick, Slow, Quick, Quick
Direction	Away from corner to centre of floor
	90 degree anti clockwise turn to next corner

How to Dance the Foxtrot

Social Foxtrot

Steps	Timing
Step	Slow
Side	Quick
Close	Quick
Side	Slow

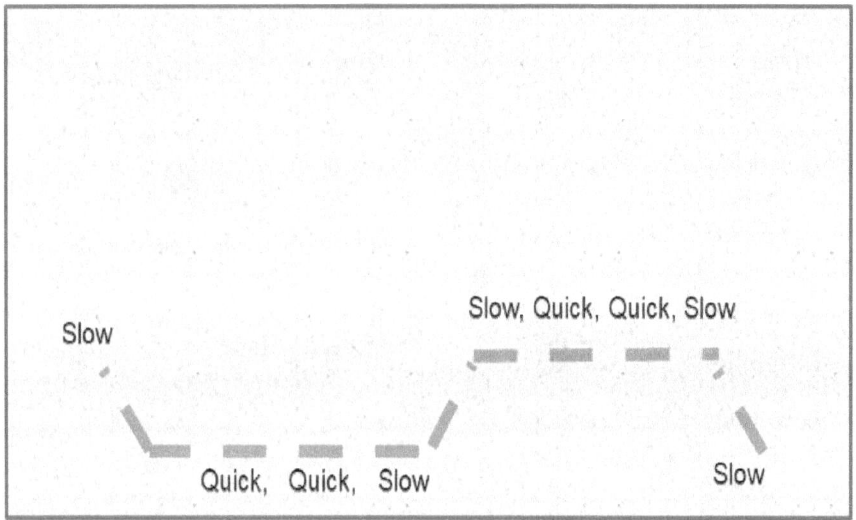

Slow Foxtrot

Key principles for dancing the Slow Foxtrot:

1. Walk as if you are going for a stroll, keep relaxed, then accentuate the steps with more up and down movement (through heel leads then rising onto the balls of your feet).
2. The foundation steps are:

- Travel a couple of steps then pause.
- 120 degree turn.
- Repeat.

3. Travel in whichever direction you like using: Slow (pause) > Quick > Quick.

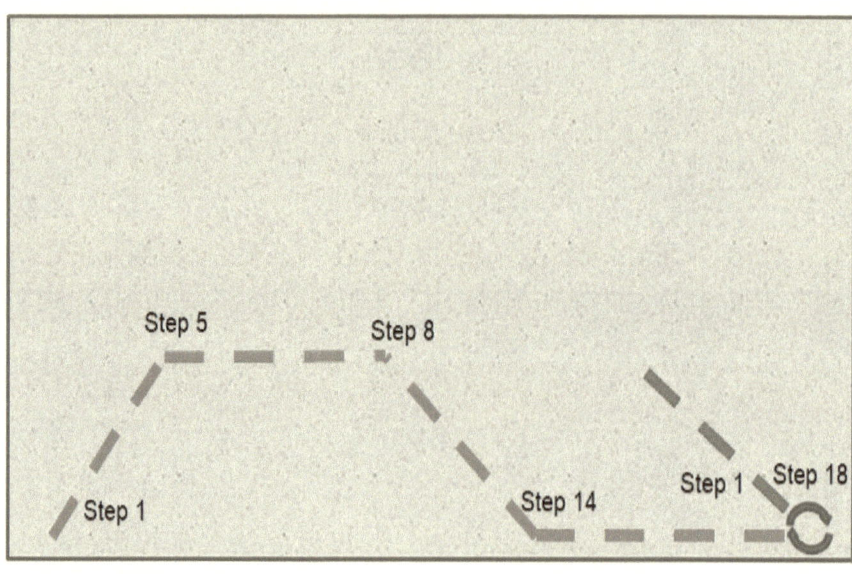

Step Number	Leader Steps	Follower Steps	Timing
1	Step forward	Step backward	Slow
2	Step forward	Step backward	Quick
3	Step forward	Step backward	Quick
4	Step forward	Step backward	Slow
5	Right side step across partner (anticlockwise)	Heel turn part 1	Quick
6	Step backward	Heel turn part 2	Quick

7	Step backward	Step forward	Slow
8	Left side step across partner (anticlockwise)	Right side step across partner (anticlockwise)	Quick
9	Step forward	Step backward	Quick
10	Step forward	Step backward	Slow
11	Step forward	Step backward	Quick
12	Step forward	Step backward	Quick
13	Step forward	Step backward	Slow
14	Left side step across partner (clockwise)	Heel turn part 1	Quick
15	Step backward	Heel turn part 2	Quick
16	Step backward	Step forward	Slow
17	Spin turn part 1	Spin turn part 1	Quick
18	Spin turn part 2	Spin turn part 2	Quick
1	Step backward from corner (60 degree turn anticlockwise to allow Follower to step across body)	Step forward	Slow
2	Step forward away from corner (60 degree turn anticlockwise to allow Follower to step across body)	Step backward	Quick

Key Principles for Dancing the Tango

1. Walk in time to the music.
2. Move like a fencer: Stand with bent knees, then extend your legs to travel.
3. The Leader moves like a stalking lion.
4. The Follower moves like a proud lioness.
5. Travel in whichever direction you want using: Slow > Slow > Quick > Quick > Slow (pause) > Quick > Quick > Slow. Or Quick > Quick > Slow (pause).

Walk like you are wearing heavy boots to get the movement of 'heel leads' ie walk forwards and step onto your heels before making contact with the ball of your foot. This applies to Leaders and Followers.

Promenade Link and Chasse

The shape this move makes is like a squashed 'T'.

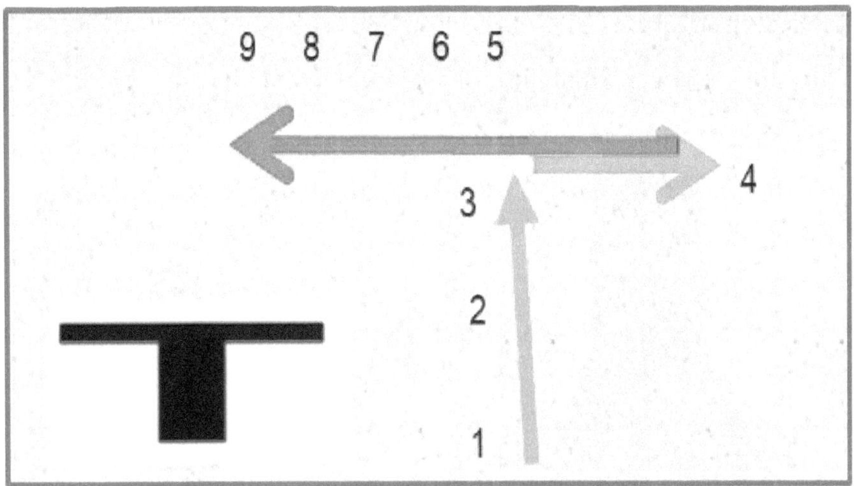

Numbers in the diagram above relate to steps in the table below

Steps	Timing	Diagram Reference
Step (to travel)	Slow	1
Step (to travel)	Slow	2
Step (to travel)	Quick	3
Side	Quick	4
Rock to side	Slow	5
Pose (weight on leg facing direction of travel)	Pause	6
Step (to travel using rear leg)	Quick	7
Side	Quick	8
Close	Slow	9

Rock Step

This move makes a shape like an upside down 'Y'.

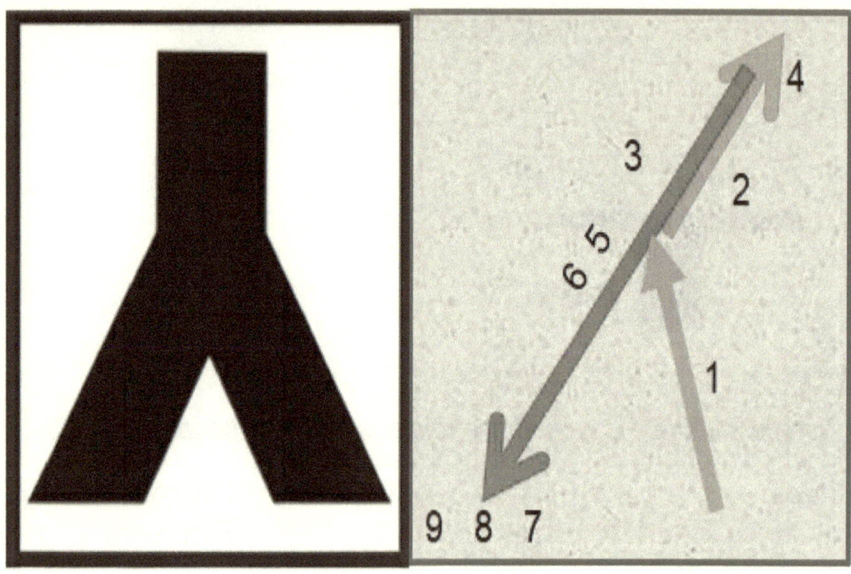

Steps	Timing	Diagram Reference
Step (to travel)	Slow	1
Step (to travel)	Slow	2
Rock on spot (Leader back, Follower forwards)	Quick	3
Rock on spot (Leader forwards, Follower back)	Quick	4
Rock on spot (Leader back, Follower forwards)	Quick	5
Pose (weight on Leader's left leg and	Pause	6

Follower's right leg)		
Step (to travel using Leader's right leg and Follower's left leg)	Quick	7
Side	Quick	8
Close	Slow	9

Chapter 5 Basic Latin Steps

On the following pages are a series of guides to get you dancing Latin steps.

- Cha Cha Cha

    - Basic Steps
    - Fan and Hockey Stick

- Jive
- Paso Doble
- Rumba
- Samba

> You can refresh your memory about framework, leading and following by looking at details in Chapter 3 before going dancing.

> Reminder: All dances start with Leader's right foot and Follower's left foot except the Jive and Tango. These start with Leader's left foot and Follower's right foot.

Cha Cha Cha Basic Steps

Key principles for dancing the Cha Cha Cha:

1. The steps are:

    - Step.
    - Rock.
    - Side.
    - Close.
    - Side.

2. The basic steps rhythm is always 2, 3, 4 and 1. This can vary in more advanced moves.

Suggested routine:

- *Basic Step.*
- *New York.*
- *Basic Step.*
- *Hand to Hand.*
- *Alemana* (underarm turn).

Basic Step (Rock Step and Chasse)

This is like going from third to second gear and back when driving a car.

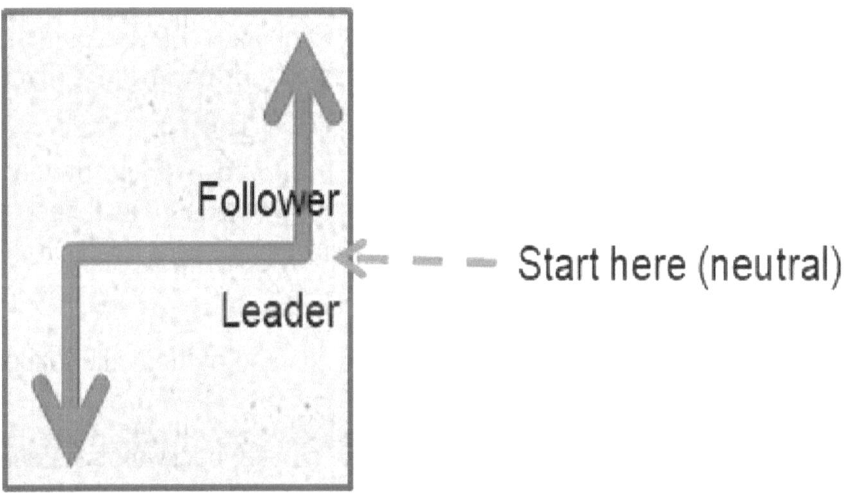

Leader: Step forward towards "third gear" > Rock back > Side > Close > Side > Step backward towards "second gear" > Rock forward > Side > Close > Side.

Follower: Step backwards towards "third gear" > Rock forward > Side > Close > Side > Step forward towards "second gear" > Rock back > Side > Close > Side.

New York Step

This is performed from a two-handed grip, instead of the usual teapot framework, whilst going side to side.

Leader: Step forward towards right side > Rock back > (Face partner) side > Close > Side > Step forward left side > Rock backward > (Face partner) side > Close > Side.

Follower: Step forward left side > Rock backward > (Face partner) side > Close > Side > Step forward towards right side > Rock back > (Face partner) side > Close > Side.

Hand to Hand Step

This is performed from a two-handed grip, instead of the usual teapot framework, whilst going side to side.

It is the mirror image off an *New York* step, so step backwards instead of forwards.

Leader: Step backward towards right side > Rock forward > (Face partner) side > Close > Side > Step backward left side > Rock forward > (Face partner) side > Close > Side.

Follower: Step backward towards left side > Rock forward > (Face partner) side > Close > Side > Step backward right side > Rock back > (Face partner) side > Close > Side.

Alemana (Underarm Turn)

This is usually done after another step eg a basic (*Rock Step* and *Chasse*).

Stay in teapot framework except for the underarm turn.

The Leader raises his/her left hand (holding Follower's right), above the Leader's left shoulder (equi-distant between Leader and Follower); and uses the Leader's right hand on Follower's left hip to help the Follower turn under the Leader's hand.

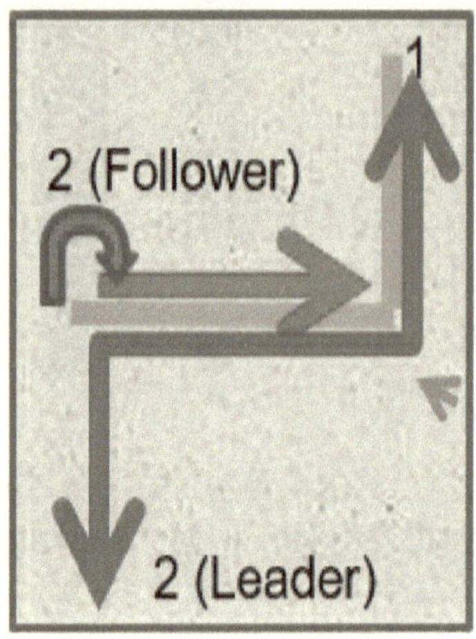

Leader: *(Basic Step (1))* step forward > Rock backward > Side > Close > Side > *(Alemana (2))* step backward, lift arm for Follower to turn under > Rock forward > Side > Close > Side.

Follower: Step backward > Rock forward > Side > Close > Side > Cross left foot over right > 360 degree clockwise turn under Leader's raised arm to face partner again > Side > Close > Side.

To improve your spins, think: Turn (beat 2) > Turn (beat 3) > Rebalance then step, step, step (beats 4 and 1).

Cha Cha Cha: Fan and Hockey Stick

Fan - Direction of Travel

Imagine a clock dial.

We will travel: Centre > 12 > Centre > 9 > Centre > 12.

Key

Red   Follower's steps

Grey   Leader's steps

Blue   Both dancers change the direction you are facing during the *Fan* move

Hints and Tips

Leader and Follower face each other unless the Leader uses the framework to point the Follower in a different direction during the turn part of a move (eg blue arrow in diagram above).

A *Hockey Stick* is like an *Alemana* (underarm turn), but goes anti-clockwise instead of clockwise. The Leader raises his/her left hand (holding Follower's right), above the Leader's right shoulder (equi-distant between Leader and Follower).

The framework is open hold, Leader's left-hand grips Follower's right hand.

Move at right angles.

Travelling in a straight line means the Leader can lead better, and Follower make sharper turns.

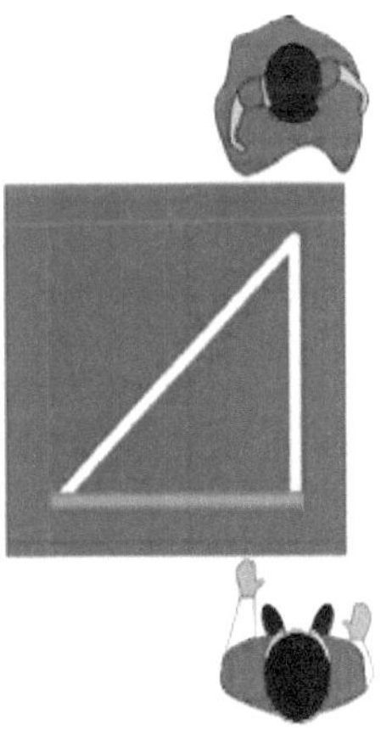

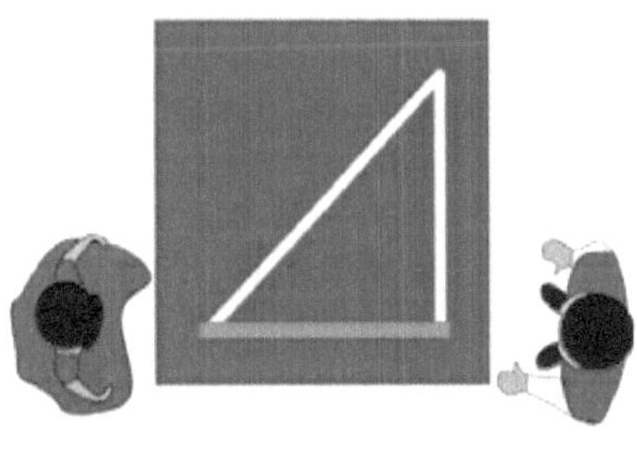

Basic Fan Steps

Timing	Leader	Follower	Move
2	Step forward	Step back	Fan
3	Rock back	Rock forward	
4 and 1	Cha Cha Cha (three steps) on spot	Forward > Lock > Forward towards the Leader	
2	Step back	45 degree step across Leader's body - facing opposite direction - (sometimes known as "*Funny Feet step 1*")	
3	Rock forward	45 degree cross step (2) to face Leader "*Funny Feet step 2*")	
4 and 1	Cha Cha Cha (side, close, side) away from the Follower	Back > Lock > Back away from the Leader	
2	Step forward (45 degree turn towards Follower)	Step together	
3	Rock back	Step forward	
4 and 1	Cha Cha Cha (side, close, side) towards the Follower	Forward > Lock > Forward towards the Leader	
2	Step back (45	Step across Leader's body	Hockey

	degree turn towards Follower)		Stick
3	Rock forward	360 degree anti-clockwise turn under Leader's raised arm to face partner again	
4 and 1	Cha Cha Cha sideways	Cha Cha Cha sideways	

Advanced Fan Steps

In the basic steps, the Follower turns her/himself during the "*Funny Feet*" steps. In the advanced steps, the Follower makes no turn until the Leader makes her/him rotate 180 degrees (on the first "*Cha*" step away from the Leader).

This new method creates a dramatic style to your dancing.

An easy way for Followers to remember direction of travel during *Cha Cha Cha Steps* (ie 4 and 1 beats):

- Straight > Straight > Straight to Leader.
- Straight > Straight > Straight from Leader.
- Straight > Straight > Straight to Leader.
- Straight > Straight > Straight from Leader.

Advanced Hockey Stick Steps

In the basic steps, the Follower *Cha Chas* sideways. In the advanced steps, the Follower can separate from the Leader (if released from the dance framework) with a back > lock > back (on the first "*Cha*" step away from the Leader). This lends itself to moves such as *the Chase*.

Timing	Leader	Follower	Move
2	Step forward	Step back	Fan
3	Rock back	Rock forward	
4 and 1	Cha Cha Cha (three steps) on spot	Forward > Lock > Forward towards the Leader	
2	Step back	Step forward	
3	Rock forward	Step forward	
4 and 1	Cha Cha Cha (side, close, side) away from the Follower	180 degree turn (to face Leader) and back > Lock > Back away from the Leader	
2	Step forward (45 degree turn towards Follower)	Step together	
3	Rock back	Step forward	
4 and 1	Cha Cha Cha (side, close, side) towards the Follower	Forward > Lock > Forward towards the Leader	
2	Step back (45 degree turn towards Follower)	Step across Leader's body	Hockey Stick

3	Rock forward	360 degree anti-clockwise turn under Leader's raised arm to face partner again	
4 and 1	(Let go of Follower's right hand) > (Step) forward > Lock > Forward towards the Follower	Back > Lock > Back away from the Leader	
2	Step forward	Step back	The Chase
3	Rock back	Rock forward	
4 and 1	Back > Lock > Back away from the Follower (facing each other)	Forward > Lock > Forward towards the Leader	
2	Step back	Step forward	
3	Rock forward	Rock back	
4 and 1	Forward > Lock > Forward towards the Follower (facing each other)	Back > Lock > Back away from the Leader	

The fastest way to get back into hold after a *Chase* is to use a *Fan* and *Alemana* (underarm turn) or *Hockey Stick* then go back into a *Basic Step (Rock Step and Chasse)* in the teapot dance framework.

A more complicated version of the *Chase* uses *Spot Turns* instead of step-rocks, and three sets of cha chas (eg Forward > Lock > Forward) in between the *Spot Turns*. I suggest trying this after you have learnt the basic version above.

Note: A *Spot Turn* is an *Alemana* without an arm to turn under, so Leaders and Followers perform the move at the same time, and both do a 360 degree turn on the spot.

Jive Basic Steps

Foot work for all basic moves: Side to Side > Side to Side > Step back from partner > Rock forwards towards partner.

Suggested routine:

- *Basic Step.*
- *Change of Place.*
- *Hand Behind the Back.*
- *Windmill.*

Basic Step (Chasse and Rock Step)

The shape this move makes is like an 'L' lying on its side.

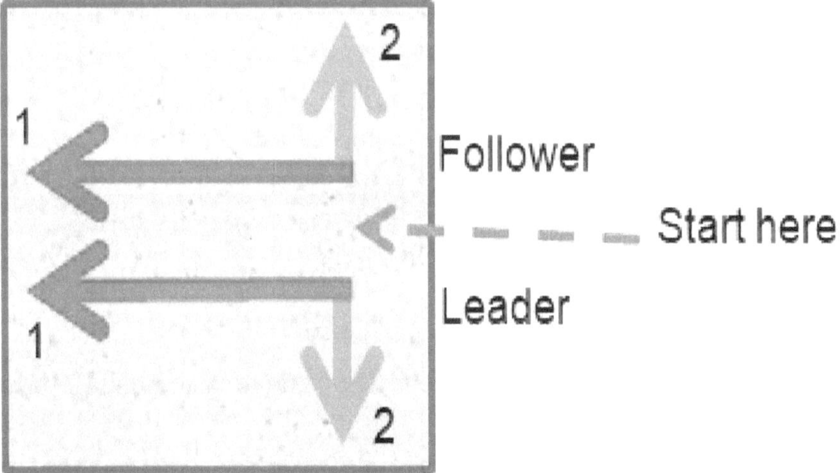

Leader: ((1) Stepping left along red arrow) side > Close > Side > (Stepping right along red arrow) side > Close > Side > ((2) Grey arrow) rock back > Step forward.

Follower: ((1) Stepping right along red arrow) side > Close > Side >

(Stepping left along red arrow) side > Close > Side > ((2) Grey arrow) rock back > Step forward.

Change of Place

The shape this move makes is like a book being opened and closed.

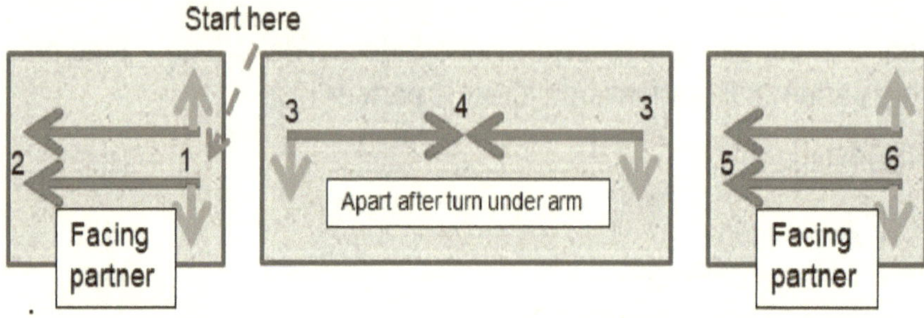

Leader: (1) Side > Close > Side ((2) lift left arm to allow Follower to pass underneath, push Follower through with right hand) > Side > Close > Side > (3) Back > Replace > Side > Close > Side ((4) lift left arm to allow Follower to pass underneath, re-join in teapot framework) > (5) Side > Close > Side > (6) Back > Replace.

Follower: (1) Side > Close > Side ((2) 180 degree clockwise turn under Leader's raised arm to face partner again) > Side > Close > Side > (3) Back > Replace > Side > Close > Side ((4) 180 degree anti-clockwise turn under Leader's raised arm to face partner again) > (5) Side > Close > Side > (6) Back > Replace.

Windmill

The shape this move makes is like a squashed 'T'.

This is performed from a two-handed grip instead of the usual teapot framework.

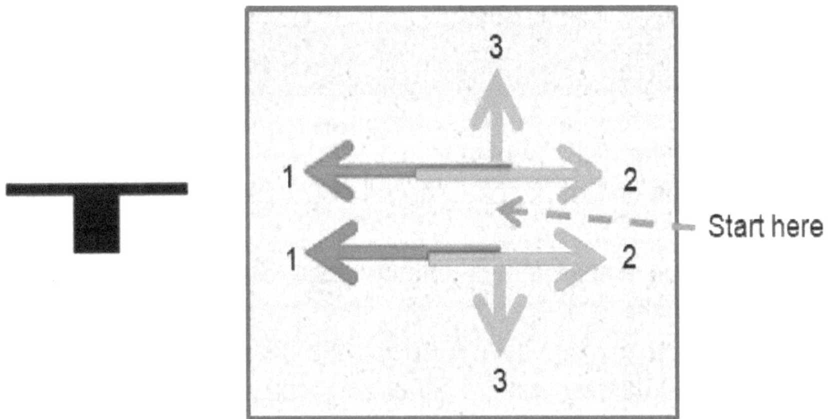

Leader and Follower: (1) Side > Close > Side > (2) Side > Close > Side > (3) Back > Replace.

Hand Behind the Back

The shape this move makes is like a chair seat.

This is performed from a one-handed grip (Leader's left and Follower's right) instead of the usual teapot framework.

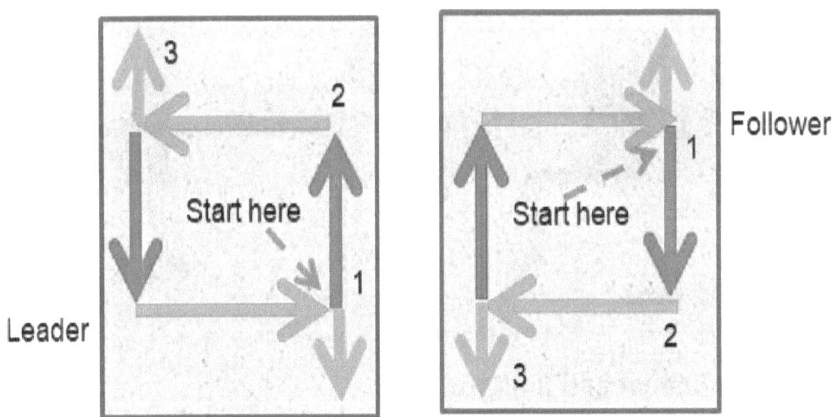

Leader and Follower: (1) Forward > Close > Forward > (Turn 90 degrees and pass hand around body then behind back) (2) Side > Close > Side > (3) Back > Replace > Repeat to return to starting position.

How to Dance the Paso Doble

Key principles:

- Walk in time to the music.
- Follow the line of dance ie go roughly corner to corner along a wall.
- Everything is done to a count of 8 beats. Start a new move when you get back to '1'.
- Suggested routine (below) follows the shape of a box. Use the 90 or 180 degree turns to either add a bit of style (to your travel around the room) or turn when you get to a corner.
- Dance as though you are a matador (Leader) flourishing a cape (Follower).

Steps for Leader and Follower	Timing (beats)
Step on spot	1 - 8
Side (to travel - Leader's right foot and Follower's left)	9

Close (Leader's left foot and Follower's right)	10
Side (to travel)	11
Close	12
Side (to travel)	13
Drag rear foot to closed position	14 - 16
Turn 180 degrees whilst stepping on spot	17 - 24
Stamp foot (Leader's right and Follower's left)	25
Walk forward (starting with Leader's left foot and Follower's right)	26 - 28
Leader walks backward whilst Follower walks forward	29 - 30
Side (to travel)	31
Close	32
Turn 90 degrees whilst stepping on spot > Start again	33 – 40

Rumba Basic Steps

Key principles for dancing the Rumba:

1. The steps are:

   - Step.
   - Rock.
   - Slide (step and drag other foot to half closed position).

2. The basic steps rhythm is always 2, 3, 4, hold (don't move on

beat 1). This can vary in more advanced moves.

Basic Step – Leader Steps Forward and Follower Backward

Follower Steps	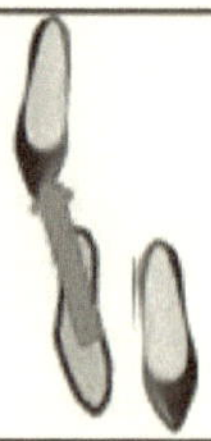		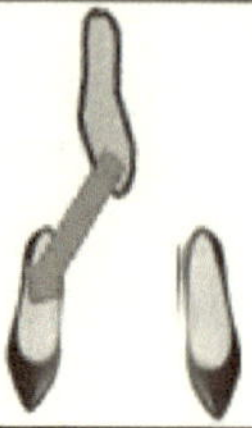	Pause
Timing	2	3	4	1
Steps	Step	Rock weight onto opposite leg	Slide leg that has no weight on it	Pause
Leader Steps				

Basic Step – Leader Steps Backward and Follower Forward

Follower Steps				Pause
Timing	2	3	4	1
Steps	Step	Rock weight onto opposite leg	Slide leg that has no weight on it	Pause
Leader Steps	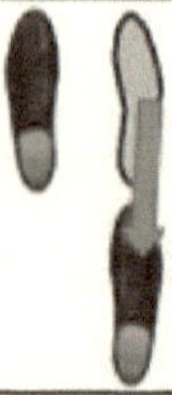		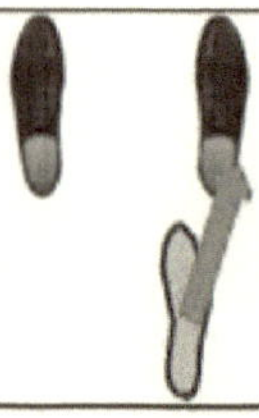	

The Rumba and Cha Cha Cha are essentially the same dance. See the Cha Cha Cha section for further details on how to do these moves.

Suggested routine:

- *Basic Step.*
- *New York.*
- *Basic Step.*
- *Hand to Hand.*
- *Alemana* (underarm turn).

You don't have to follow the moves in the order above, you can fit them together in different combinations.

Basic Step – Advanced Version

To get a more sensual movement in your dance (remember: Rumba is the dance of love), the timing can be changed to 2-and-3-and-4-and-1. This applies to both Leaders and Followers. Your Rumba will now be slightly faster and have more hip movement to make it look more like Salsa in style.

The Leader will look strong and proud. The Follower will look desirable and will spend the dance teasing (ie playing hard to get) the Leader who will be trying to win over the Follower.

Samba Basic Steps

Key principles for dancing the Samba:

1. Find your inner bounce.
2. The foundation steps are:

    - Step (travelling).
    - Bounce (on spot).
    - Bounce (on spot).

3. The foundation rhythm is: Slow > Quick > Quick. Like a heartbeat: Dum, dum-dum.

To get yourself up and dancing the Samba just use: Step > Side > Close.

- The step is a small jump as though you are stepping over a 30cm hole in the ground.
- The Side > Close is on the spot where you land from the step.
- Rhythm: 1-a-2, 2-a-2.

Direction	Leader Steps	Follower Steps
	Forward and back in a straight line.	Forward and back in a straight line.
Round and round in anti-clockwise circle.	Straight forward, then turn roughly 45 degrees when going backwards.	Straight backwards, then turn roughly 45 degrees when going forward.

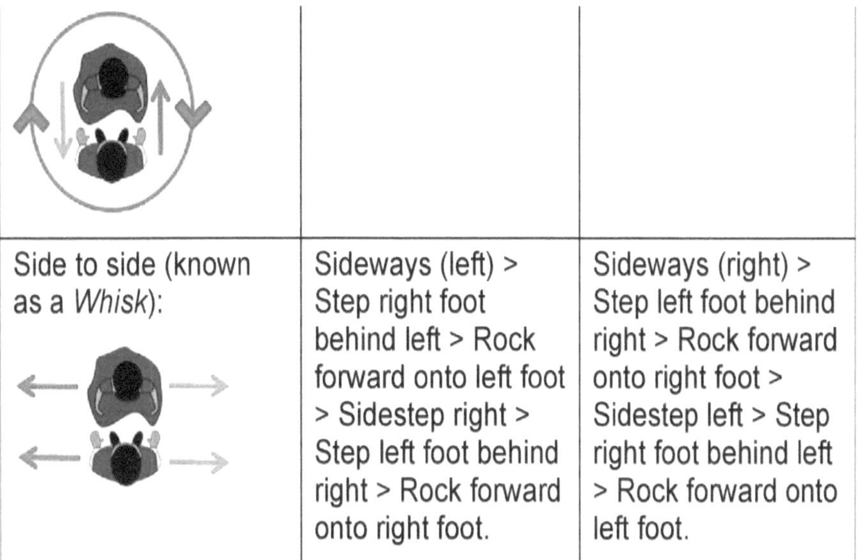

Side to side (known as a *Whisk*):	Sideways (left) > Step right foot behind left > Rock forward onto left foot > Sidestep right > Step left foot behind right > Rock forward onto right foot.	Sideways (right) > Step left foot behind right > Rock forward onto right foot > Sidestep left > Step right foot behind left > Rock forward onto left foot.

More advanced steps (eg *Samba Walk*) will require different footwork to the foundation steps.

Chapter 6 More Advanced Ballroom Steps

The next chapter will help you with more advanced Ballroom steps.

- Double Reverse Spin – Waltz
- How to Dance Natural Pivots

Double Reverse Spin – Waltz

Double Reverse Spins are usually performed in combination with other moves eg *Introduction Move > Double Reverse Spin > Exit Move.*

Double Reverse Spins are not hard moves! You just have to do some basic moves (one after another) faster.

Think of it like this: You have nine beats to do a *Reverse Turn* and *Change Step* in the Waltz. This takes you around in a full circle and allows you to recover (ie straighten up) before doing a new move after a turn.

A *Reverse Spin* requires you to do something like a *Reverse Turn* and recovery move in three beats. Do one *Reverse Turn* after another (turn > recover > turn > recover) and you have a *Double Reverse Spin*. Easy when you know how!

> If you want to do two *Natural Spins*, you can use the idea above to go clockwise rather than anti-clockwise. This one principle has two uses.

Suggested Routine

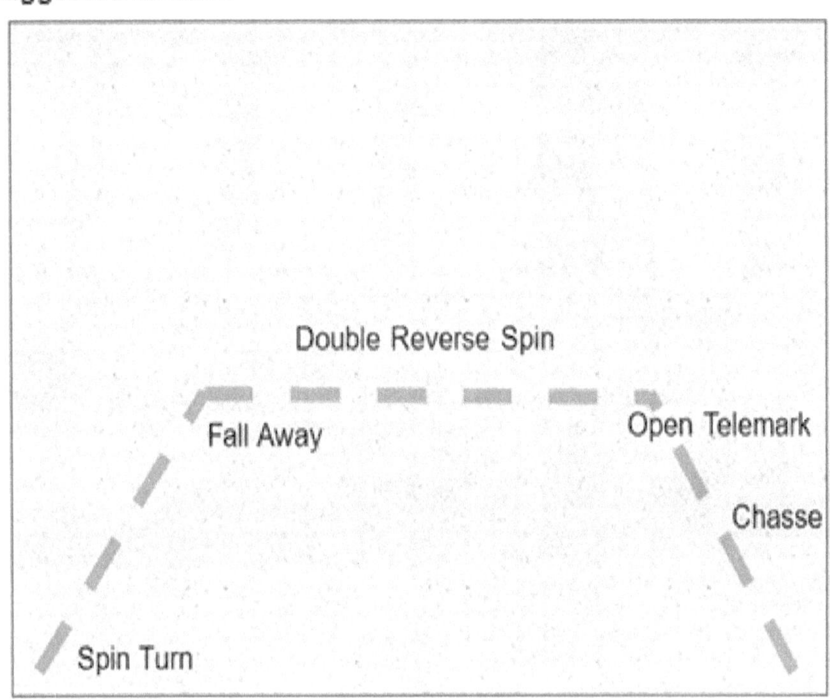

Direction of Travel

Leader: Moves (roughly) in a straight line.

Follower: Moves around the Leader whilst maintaining three points of contact in ballroom framework.

The steps should be performed in a space you can travel within two footsteps.

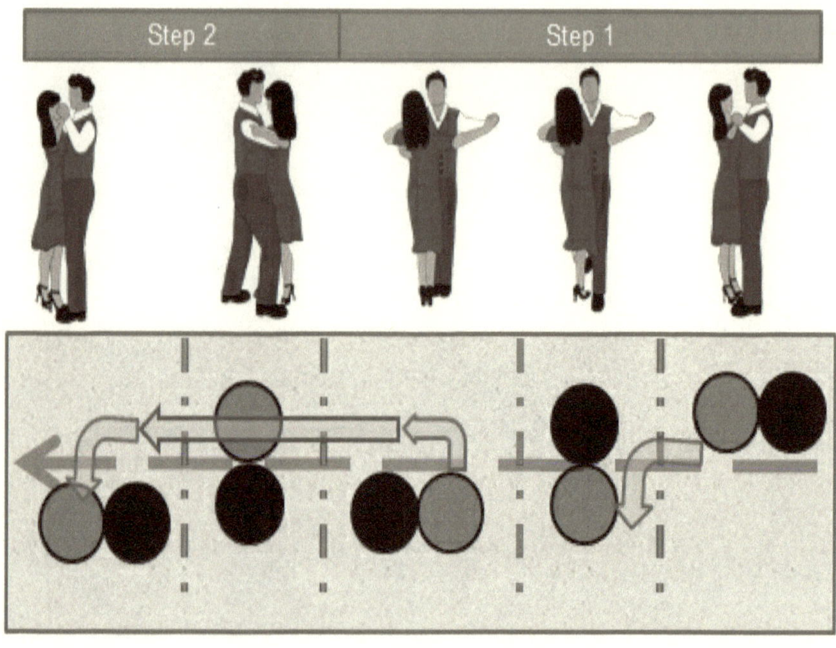

Key: Leader: Black dots   Follower: Grey dots

Line: Different steps   Arrow: Direction of travel

Leader Steps

Step	Direction	Timing
Forward heel turn	90 degree turn	Beat 1
Close feet	90 degree turn	Beat 2
Step back left foot so it is behind right, like in the *Whisk (to allow follower to pass)*		Beat 2.5
Spot turn and close feet	180 degree	Beat 3

	turn	

Follower Steps

Step	Direction	Timing
Heel turn (part 1)	90 degree turn facing Leader	Beat 1
Heel turn (part 2)	90 degree turn facing Leader	Beat 2
Step forward	Straight towards Leader, but stepping to side so Follower's left hip is in contact with Leader's left hip	Beat 2.5
Cross step	180 degree turn to face Leader	Beat 3

Note: Most of the 180 degree turn is done in the cross step, really turn your hips like a Cha Cha Cha *Alemana Turn*.

An easy way to remember: Turn, turn, step, turn.

> If learning the *Double Reverse Spin* seems hard, just remember:
>
> - You are not learning new steps….
> - You are just joining together a bit of **Foxtrot** and **Viennese Waltz**.

Double Reverse Spin – Foxtrot Part

Do you remember steps 5 and 6 from the Foxtrot – heel turn and step? This is part one of a reverse spin (beats 1 and 2).

Double Reverse Spin – Viennese Waltz Part

Do you remember "Leader crosses" > "Follower crosses" steps from the Viennese Waltz? The Follower uses these cross steps from the

Reverse Turn to step past the Leader. This is part two of a reverse spin (beats 2.5 and 3).

How to Dance Natural Pivots

Key principles:

- *Pivots* are a series of steps in a circular direction.
- Keep feet roughly shoulder width apart when moving.
- Step: Heel > Toe (ie ball of foot) > Heel > Toe etc.
- Keep down low for balance, there is no rise and fall when you alternate stepping on heels and toes.
- Both dance partners need to help each other to do *Pivots*. Each party will have to rotate around the other to keep up momentum. The Leader starts the move, by helping the Follower around him/her. The Follower needs to complete the *Pivot*, by helping the Leader around him/her.
- If only one party provides the momentum, you will not get enough turn and end up going the wrong way around the dance floor ie back into other dancers (instead of away from them).

Direction of Travel

Direction of travel is anti-clockwise by stepping clockwise.

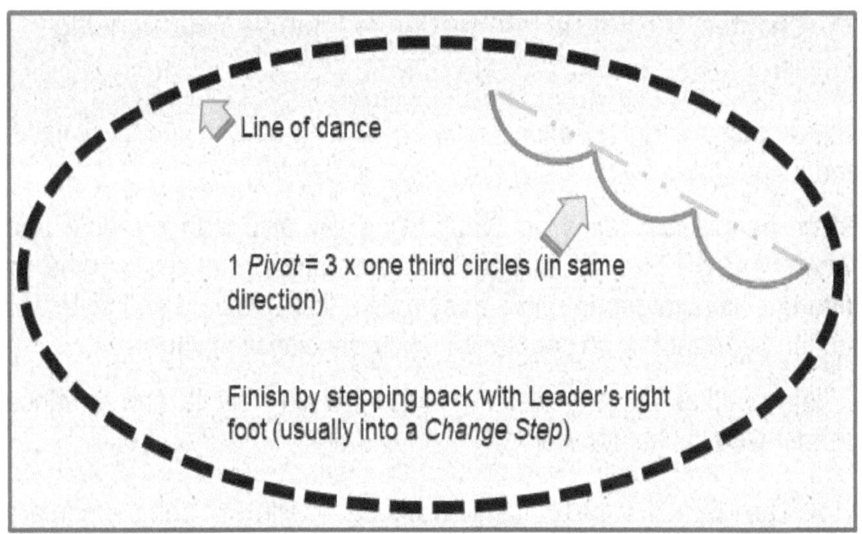

It is possible to travel in a complete circle, but normal to use *Pivots* to travel partially around the dance floor eg one quarter.

Footwork

Steps:

- Leader: Heel > Toe > Heel > Toe etc.
- Follower: Toe > Heel > Toe > Heel etc.

Chapter 7 Technical Information to Improve Your Dancing

The next chapter gives information on how to improve your technique, and so progress from a beginner to expert dancer.

Some people just focus on 'what' to do. By also learning 'how' and 'when' you will be able to progress by combining moves together in different ways to get around a busy dance floor. Also, to add style and fun to your dancing, so people will enjoy dancing with you!

In this chapter there is also some advice on how to find a dance partner who is right for you.

- The Benefits of Finding Someone With a Complementary Learning Style?
- Sequence Versus Leading and Following
- Progressing From Beginner to Expert Dancer

The Benefits of Finding Someone With a Complementary Learning Style

The situation:

- You are at a dance class (without a regular partner).
- You find someone to dance with.
- You start practising moves together.
- Things don't go well and you ask yourself why?

   Answer: You may both learn in different ways. This can cause conflict unless you make allowances for each other's learning styles. Things to look out for and options to avoid conflict are listed on the next few pages.

If you are going to dance lessons on your own try to find someone in class with a learning style you can get along with.

This will avoid conflict and help you get the most from your dance lessons.

Regular partners may experience conflict if they both learn in different ways. Allow each other time to absorb and then use what you have learned in classes according to your own preferred learning style. One person should not dominate the partnership.

Remember your roles! (See Chapter 3.) There can only be one Leader and one Follower. Don't do the other person's job instead of your own.

People learn and progress in different ways and at different rates by:

- Listening.
- Watching.
- Doing.

Some people like an overview whereas others want detail.

- Overview Style: Learns lots of general information quickly. Learns detail later.
- Detail Style: Learns a couple of things at a time, but in a lot of detail.

The two learning styles complement each other more when both parties have some experience to use/share.

When working with a partner, you may have to adapt to someone else's learning style, and them to yours. Particularly if their learning style is markedly different to yours. It becomes clear as one dances whether the partnership works or not.

There may be some initial conflict until each party recognises the other works/learns in a different way.

Why not discuss:

- What steps you both want to dance.
- Order of steps.

- How to do steps.

The key to successful/enjoyable dancing is that two people work together as one unit.

If your partner has a different learning style to you, why not try dancing with other (more experienced) partners some of the time?

Sequence Versus Leading and Following

I have noticed dancers have two distinct learning styles:

1. Learning moves as a sequence.
2. Leading and following.

Each style has advantages and disadvantages.

Sequence

- Focus on 'what' to do.
- A quick way to learn fixed routines.
- Dancers have to learn new routines to vary the order of moves.
- Each partner needs to learn the same routine. Dancers can only dance with someone who knows their routine.

Leading and Following

- Focus on:

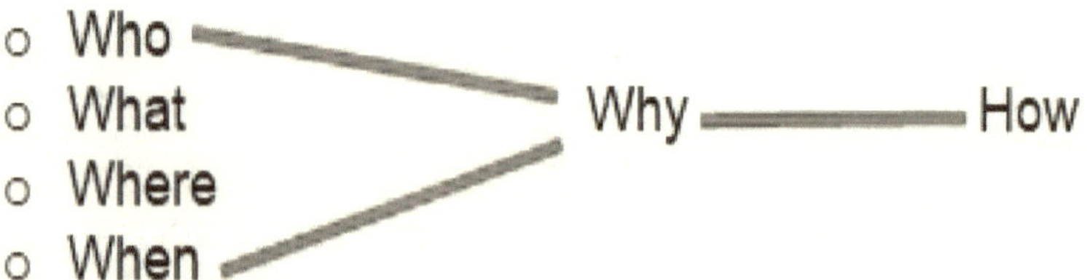

- Takes time to learn, but dancers can then vary combinations of moves instead of learning fixed routines.

- Dancers can dance with anyone who can lead or follow.

Progressing From Beginner to Expert Dancer

Beginner	Intermediate	Advanced
Learns individual moves	Looks for patterns to learn faster by understanding that a 'new' technique is similar to, or is, one learnt previously but now used in a different way	Combines individual moves in different ways by leading or following

> Note that often what looks like a complicated move is in fact a combination of two or more beginner (or intermediate) moves.

Several (eg three) beginner moves can be combined into one intermediate move, and several (eg three) intermediate moves can be combined into one advanced move. This will affect timing and requires component moves to be done faster. For example a Waltz *Natural Turn* and *Change Step* takes nine beats, but a *Spin Turn* (practically the same movement) takes three.

(Numbers in this table are a guide to step combinations).

<table>
<tr><td colspan="3"></td><td colspan="3" align="center">1</td><td colspan="3"></td><td>Advanced</td></tr>
<tr><td colspan="3" align="center">1</td><td colspan="3" align="center">2</td><td colspan="3" align="center">3</td><td>Intermediate</td></tr>
<tr><td>1</td><td>2</td><td>3</td><td>4</td><td>5</td><td>6</td><td>7</td><td>8</td><td>9</td><td>Beginner</td></tr>
</table>

Doing a basic move with style makes it look more advanced than it actually is. For example, it is possible to combine a basic Leader forwards step with a Follower's sideways step to get the Follower travelling in a different direction to the Leader. This occurs in the *Wing* in the Waltz. Here the Leader takes one step forward (45 degrees to line of dance) on beat 1 then pauses for beats 2 and 3; the Follower walks around the front of the Leader (maintaining three points of contact in ballroom hold) from the Leader's right to left hip on beats 1 – 3.

Through leading and following, it is possible to change the combinations of moves. This variation would not be possible if they were taught as a sequence, as a new sequence would need to be learnt every time a change was desired.

Dancers need to learn signals given by the Leader to the Follower which indicate a particular step is coming next. (See Chapter 3.)

There are only a limited number of key moves to learn, but there can be many variations on these. By learning the key moves (eg *Spin Turn*) you can apply these as different techniques. For example, having learnt the *Spin Turn* in the Waltz, you can then use it in the Quickstep. Do remember that different dances may use the same move but use different timing. For example, the *Weave* is six steps (beats) in the Waltz; but in Tango is quick, quick, slow, quick, quick, slow.

Dedication

To my teachers

Jo Murray-Watson

For getting me into dancing
which is now a long term passion

Graeme Hein-Jones

Strictly Dance (Linton)

For keeping me interested in
dancing and improving my
technique

Richard Drage

Ickleton Judo Club

For teaching me to be a better student, and to see the patterns
linking dancing and martial arts

Acknowledgements

Susanna West Yates

As editor in chief – thank you for all your help and support.

Nicola Harvey

Nicky, without you, Graeme's classes would be like being taught by Morecambe without Wise; or Fred without Ginger.

Proof Readers

Thank you for all your proof reading: Hilary, Eva, Heike, Dave, Jan, John, Tris, Janet and Leslie.

Artist's Models for Book Illustrations

Thank you for all your help: Rachel, David, Sarah, Tony, Graeme, Nicky, Julie, Kathy, Helen and Wanda.

Eve Moesis

Thank you for your patience and attention to detail when illustrating the figures in this book.